A Trilogy of
Illustrated Poems

COMPOSTING TEMPLES

rm mist

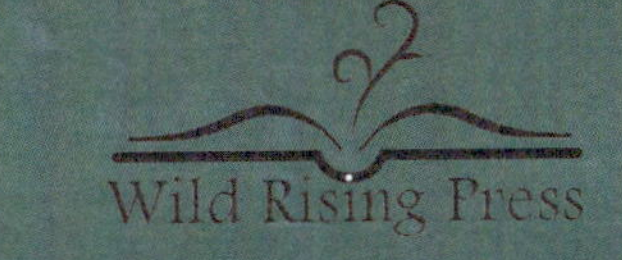

EVERGREEN, COLORADO

Artwork: rm mist
Editor: Judyth Hill
Book Design: Mary Meade
www.wildrisingpress.com

First Edition
ISBN 978-1-957468-54-9

I dedicate this trilogy to death doulas and others who kindly hold space for us as we make our return to the holy.

Contents

Preface

Temple (n) —a place devoted to a special purpose
Compost (n)—a mixture that consists of largely decayed organic matter.
Compost (v)—to convert to compost
—Merriam Webster Dictionary

Humans are a funny species,
stacking stones to house the sacred and divine,
a place to visit the holy.

We are a clever species,
gathering dross to enrich the gardens.
We are a curious species,
asking what if every life is a temple?
Each body devoted to change/to creation with its own divinity.

Asking what if
the holy flows in and flows out of us too?
In and out of all life,
the sacred finding new purpose for its trash,
composting drek for the next temple?

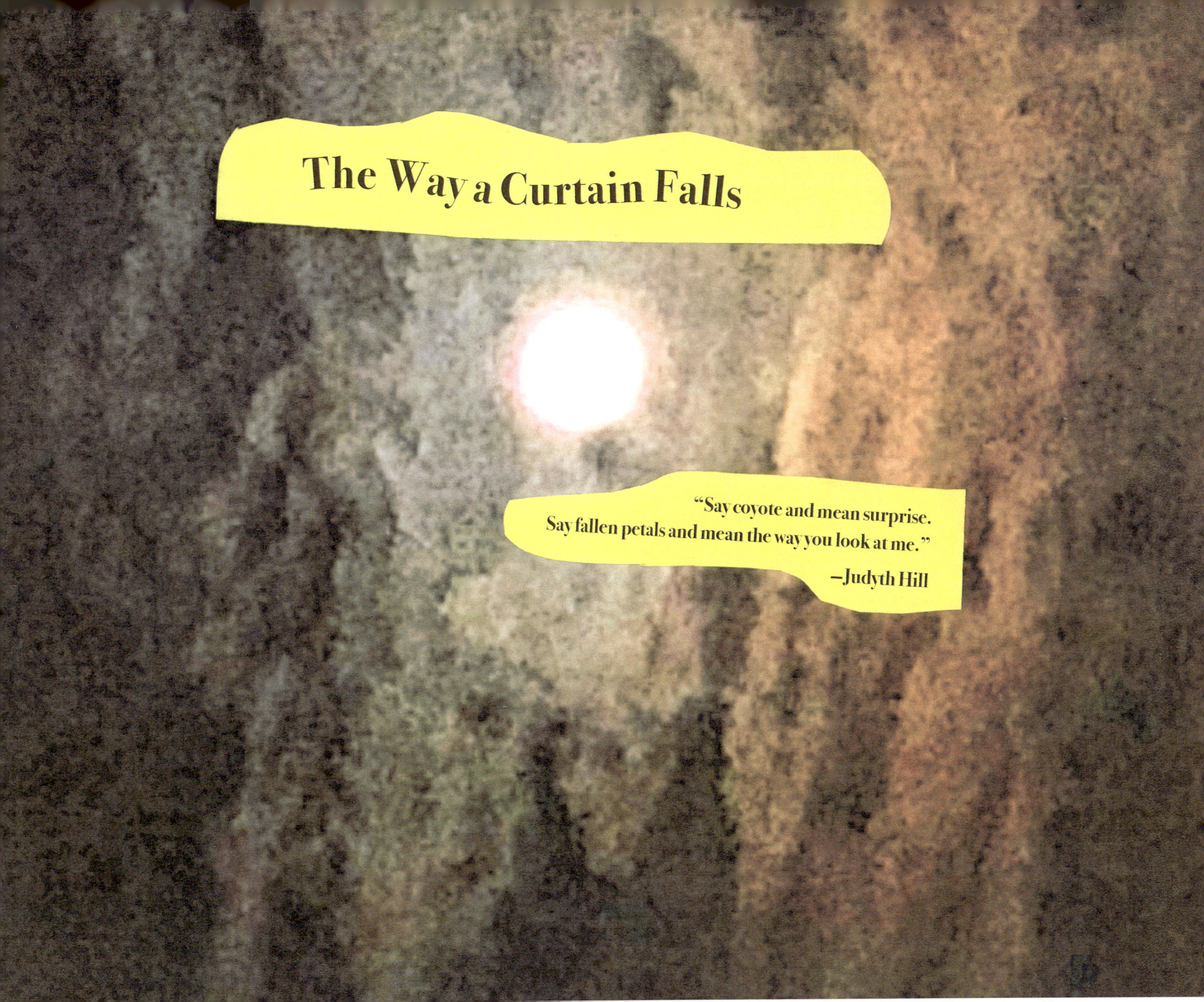
The Way a Curtain Falls
"Say coyote and mean surprise.
Say fallen petals and mean the way you look at me."
—Judyth Hill

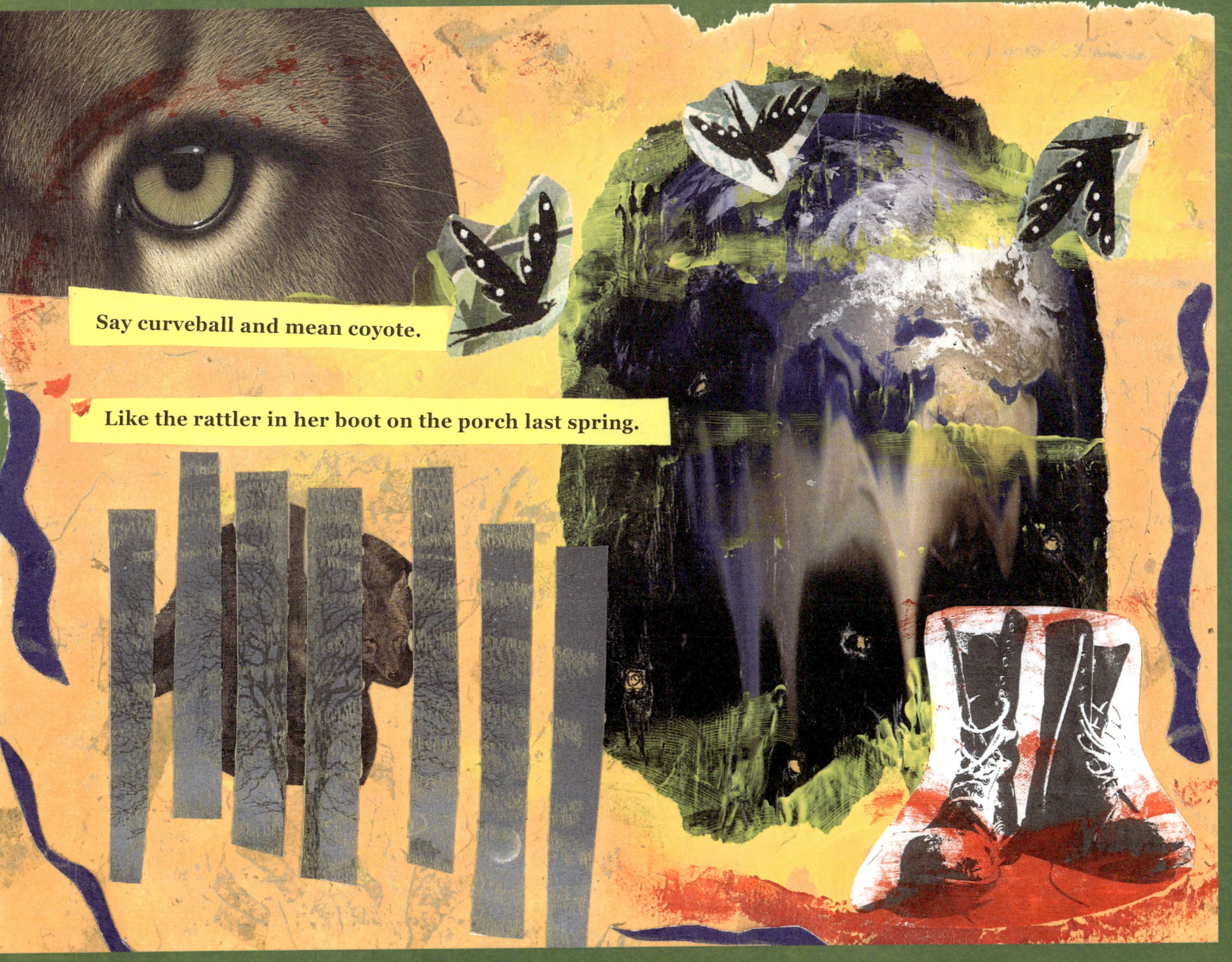
Say curveball and mean coyote.
Like the rattler in her boot on the porch last spring.

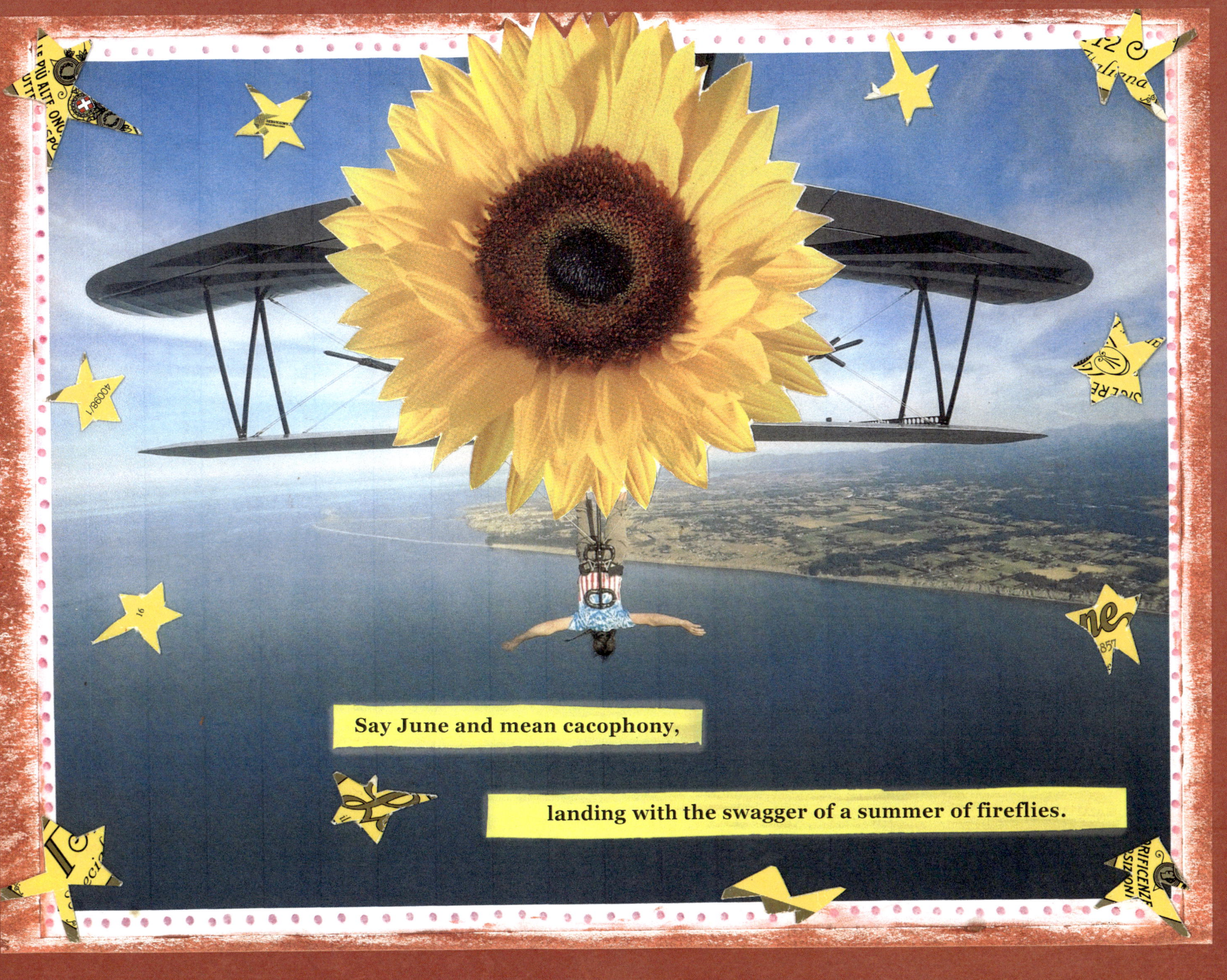
Say June and mean cacophony,
landing with the swagger of a summer of fireflies.

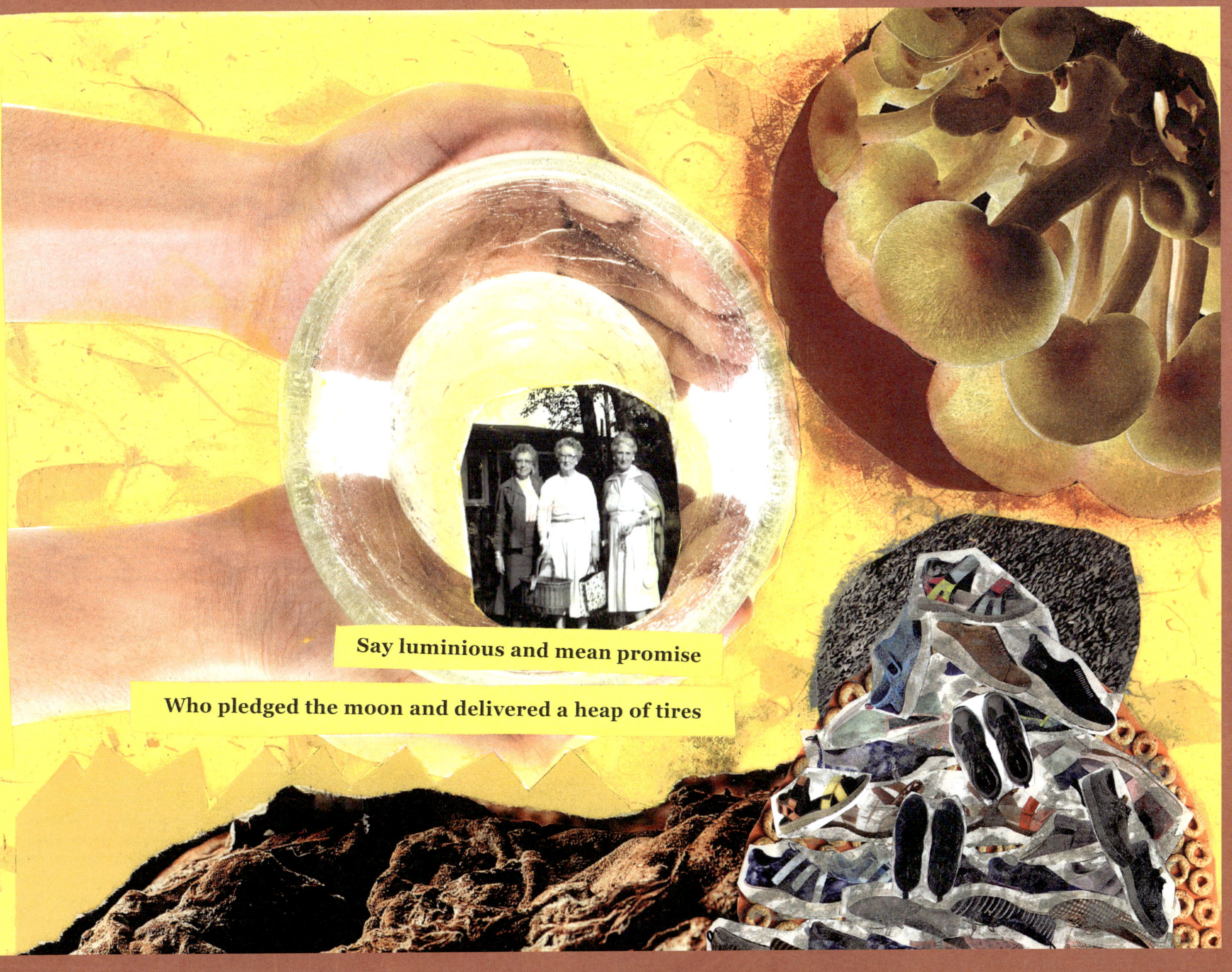
Say luminious and mean promise
Who pledged the moon and delivered a heap of tires

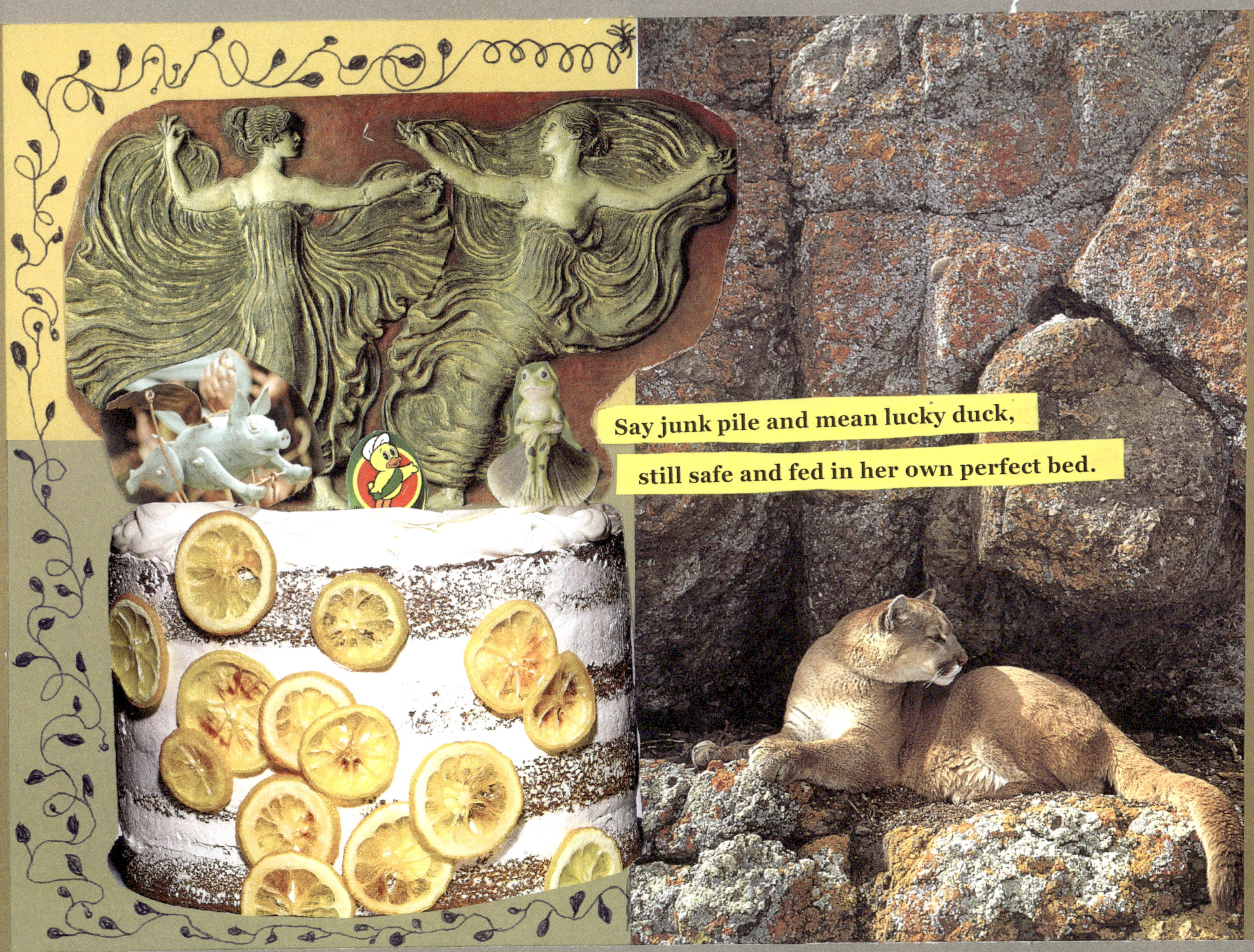
Say junk pile and mean lucky duck,
still safe and fed in her own perfect bed.

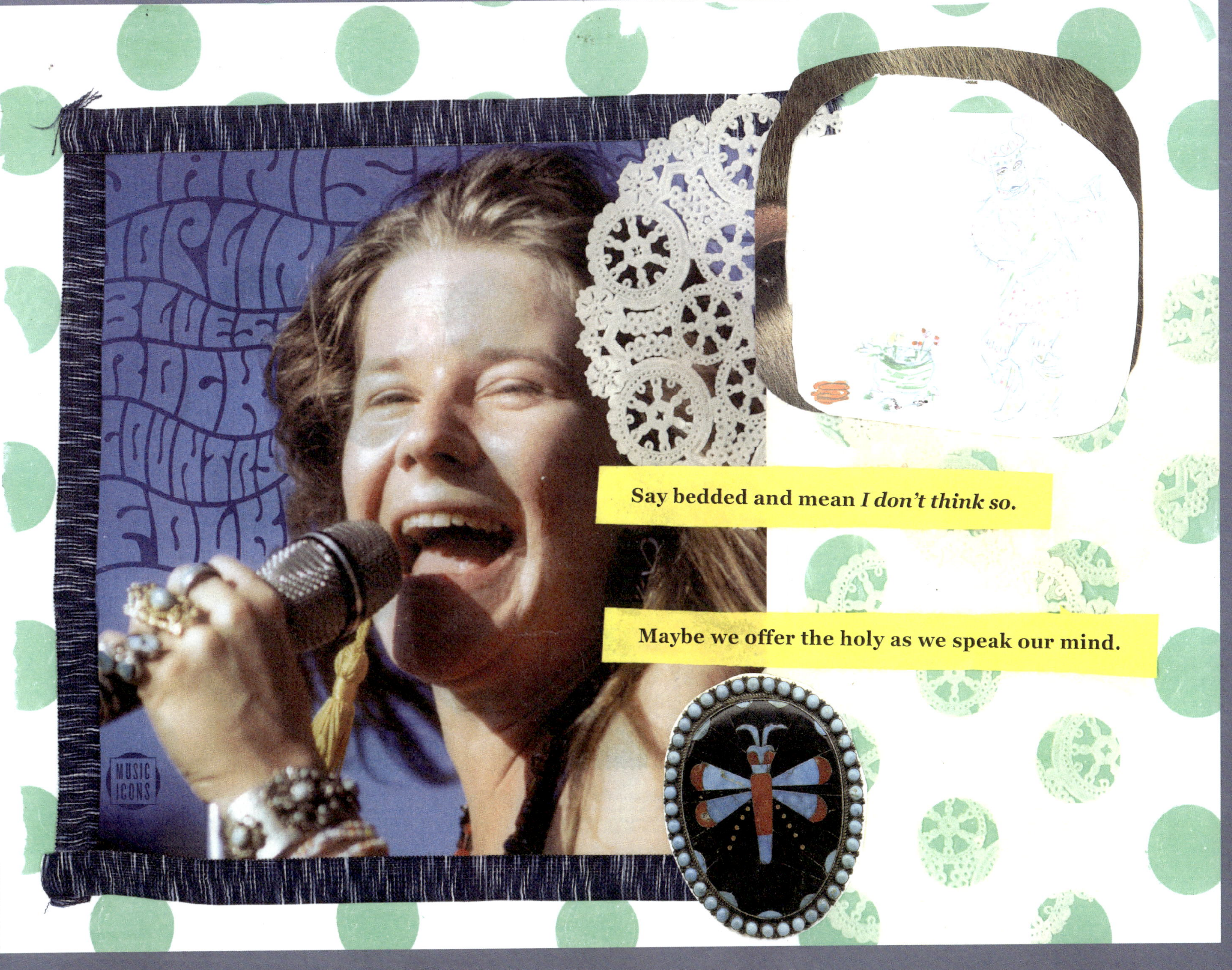
Say bedded and mean *I don't think so.*
Maybe we offer the holy as we speak our mind.
MUSIC
ICONS

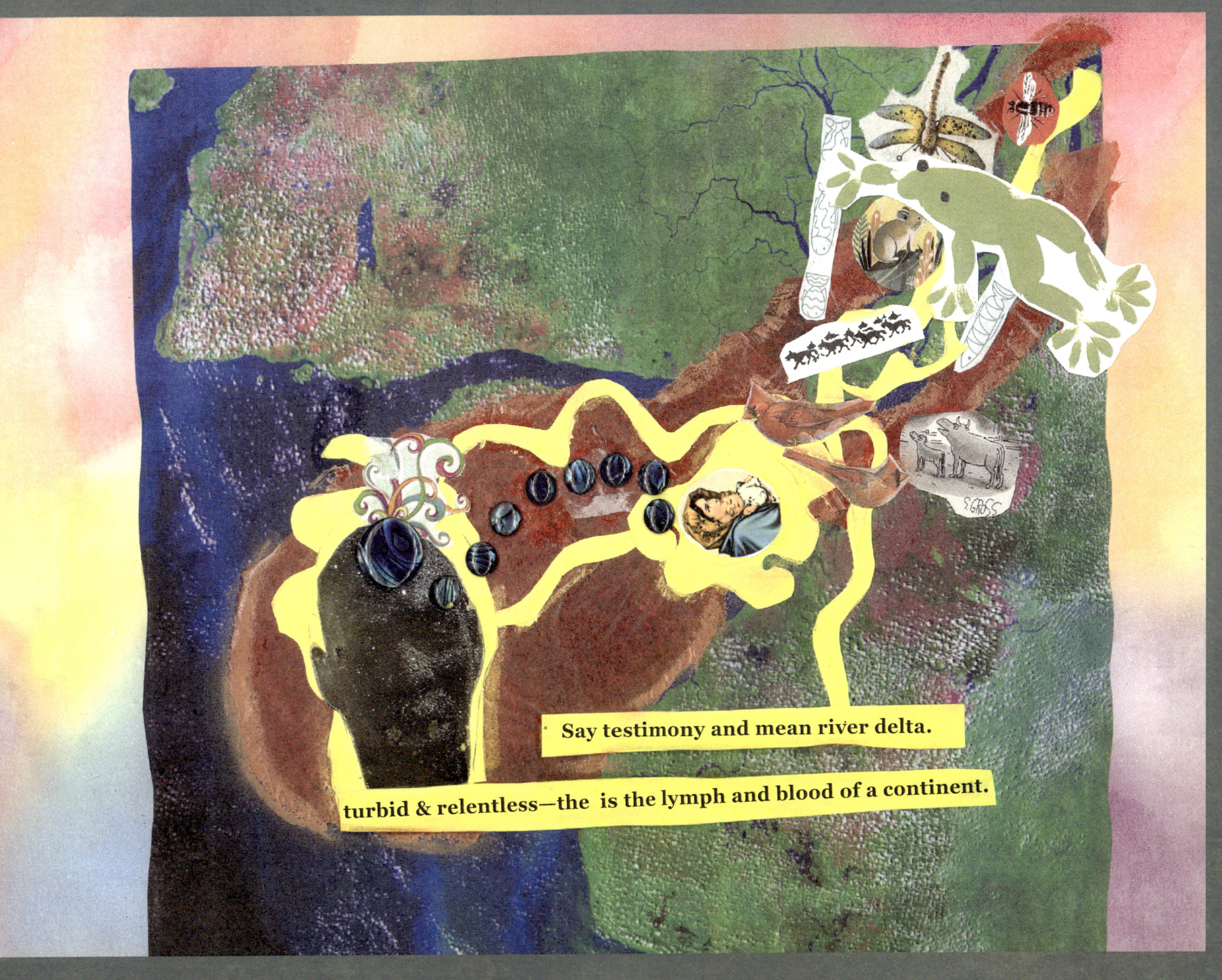
S.GROSS
Say testimony and mean river delta.
turbid & relentless—the is the lymph and blood of a continent.

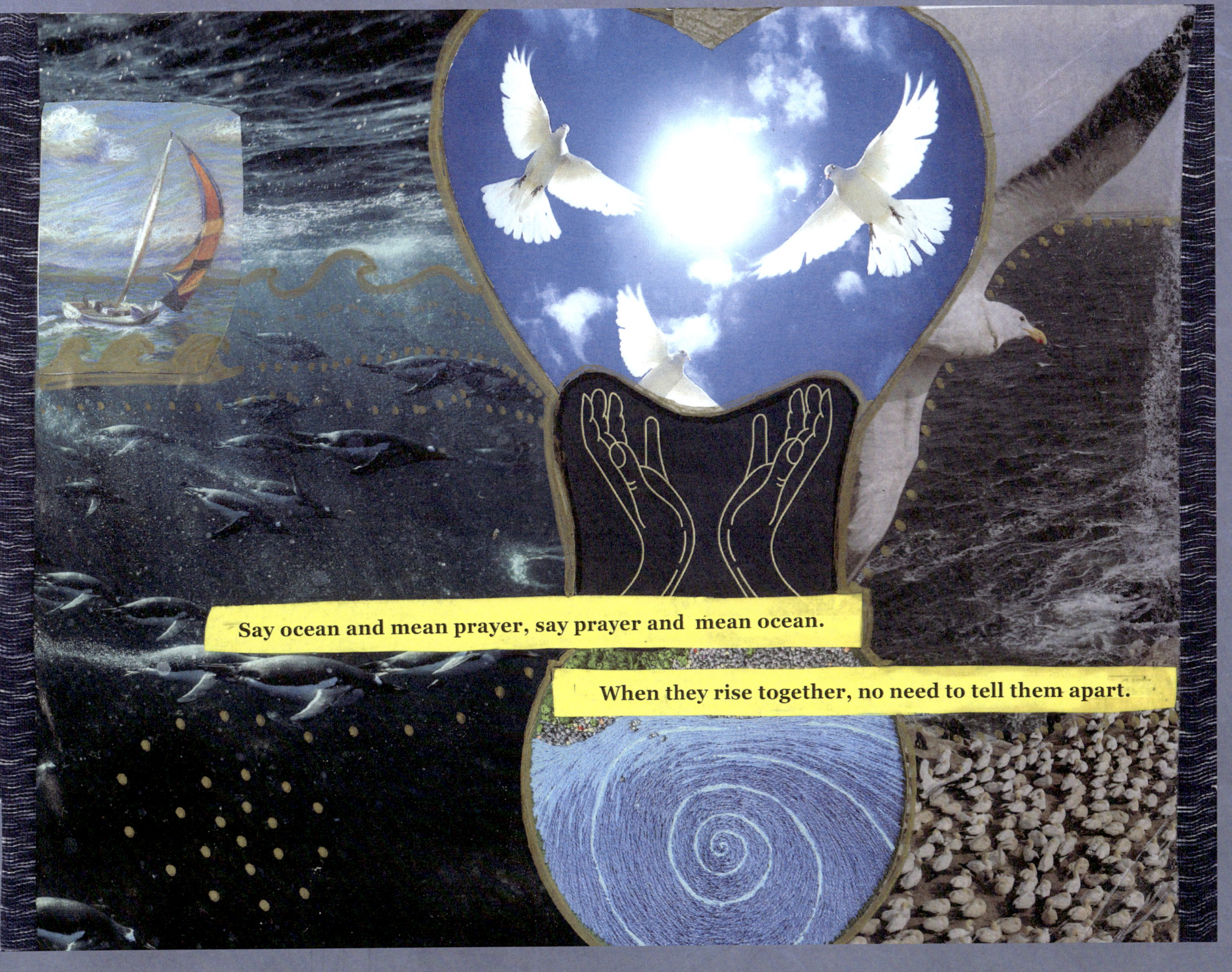
Say ocean and mean prayer, say prayer and mean ocean.
When they rise together, no need to tell them apart.

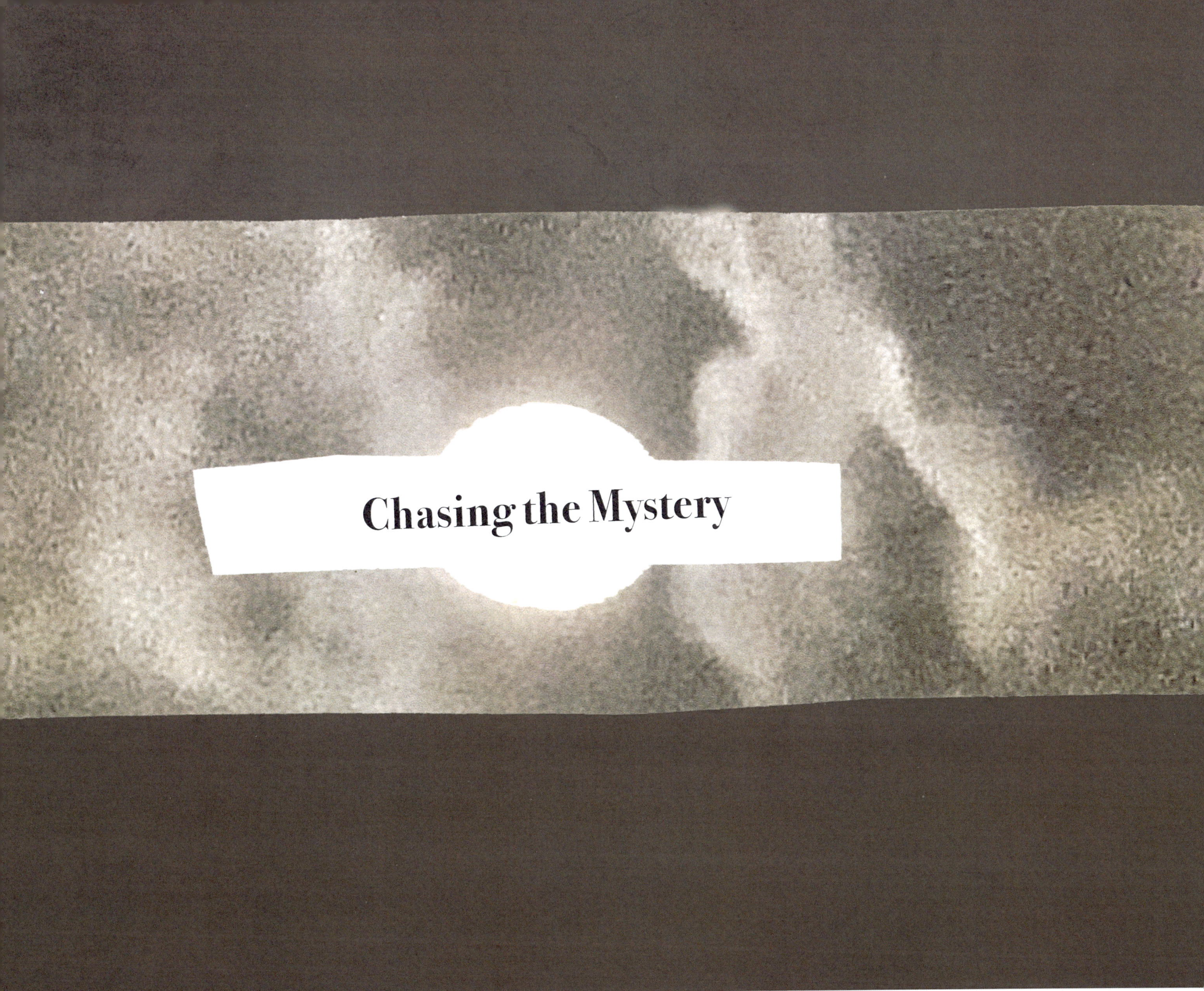

Chasing the Mystery

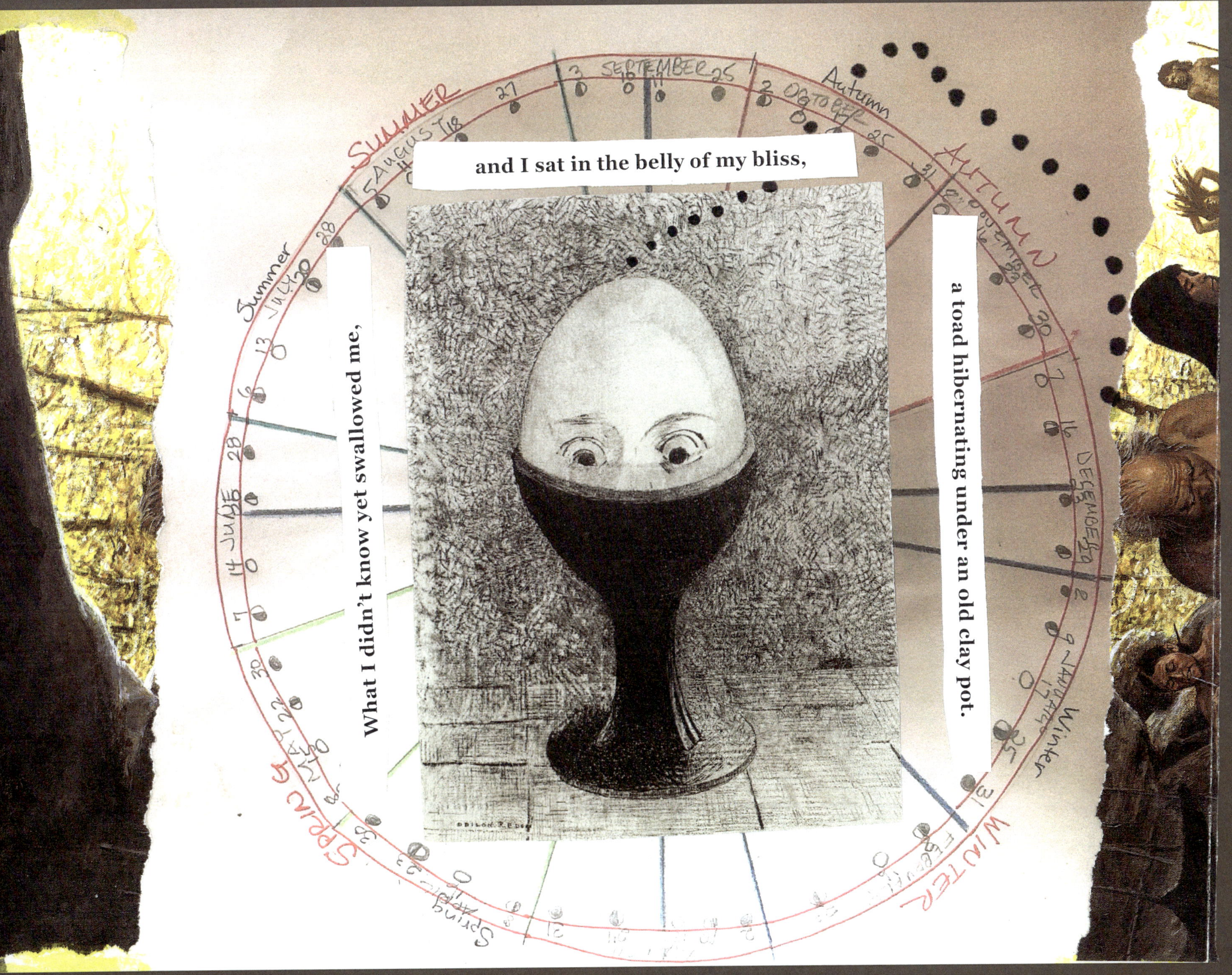
What I didn't know yet swallowed me,
and I sat in the belly of my bliss,
a toad hibernating under an old clay pot.
SUMMER
AUTUMN
WINTER
SPRING

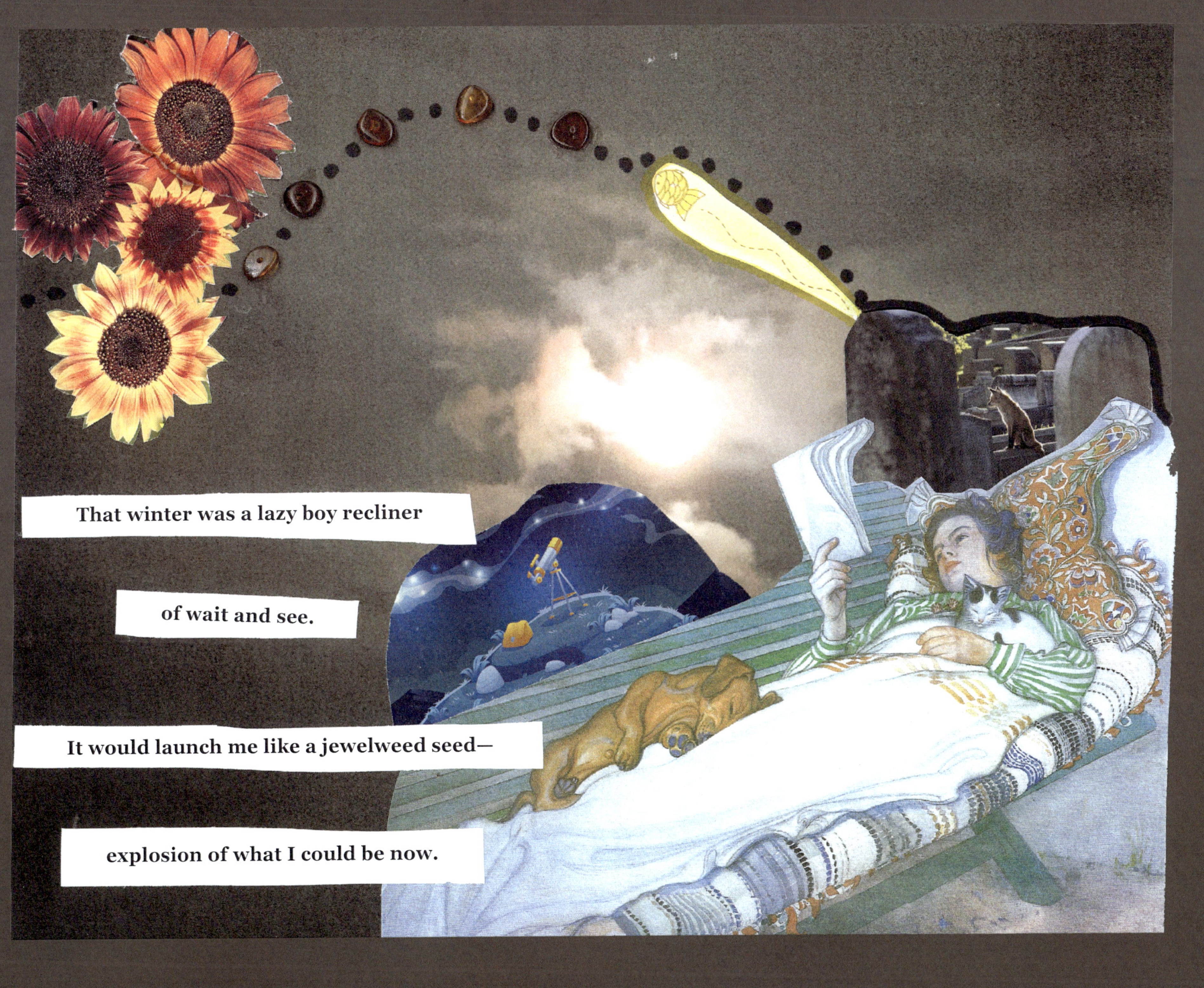
That winter was a lazy boy recliner
of wait and see.
It would launch me like a jewelweed seed—
explosion of what I could be now.

30

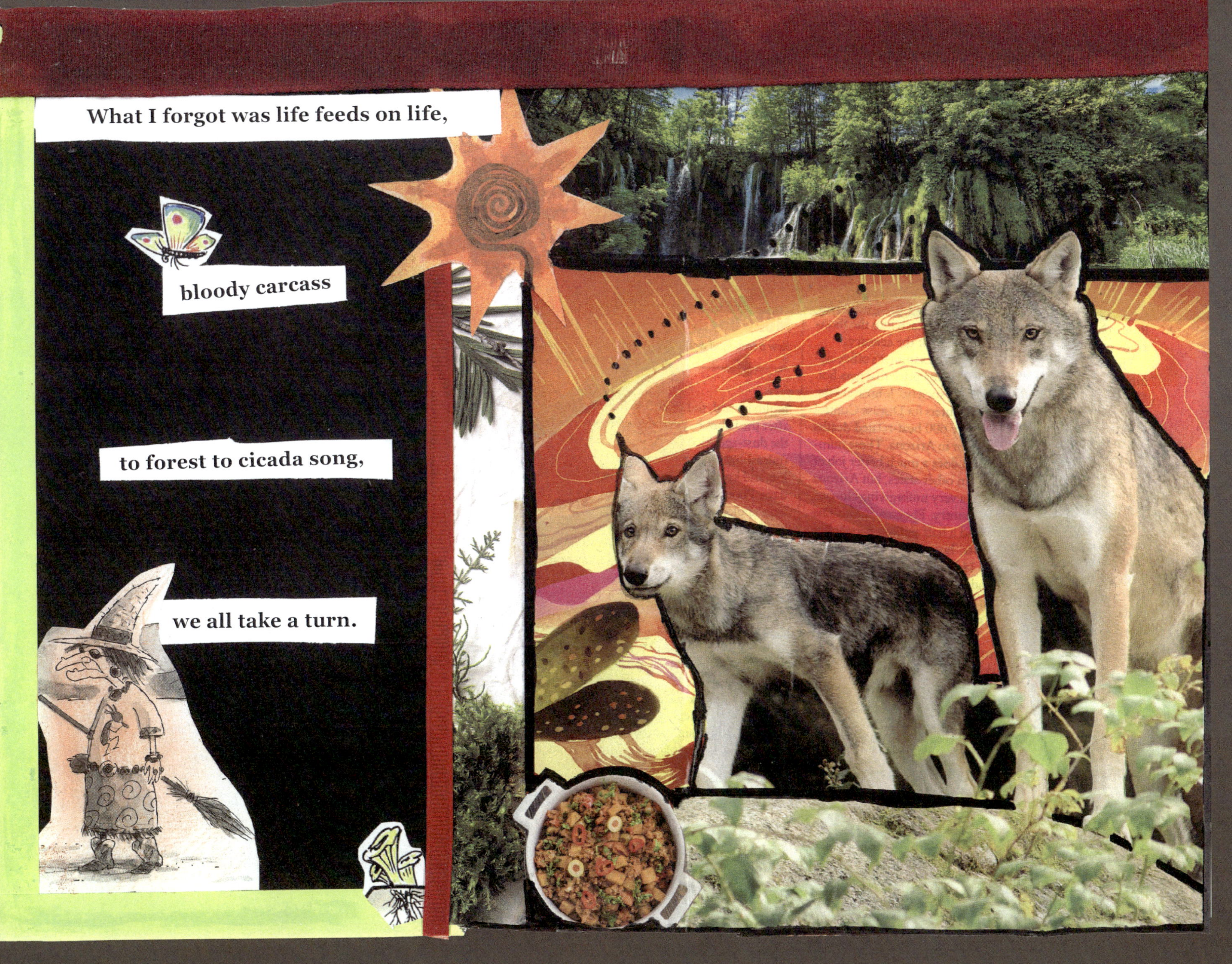
What I forgot was life feeds on life,
bloody carcass
to forest to cicada song,
we all take a turn.

What I believed was mercy

is a red blanket, permeable,

frayed along the edges,

sometimes spreading wide as

the Mississippi, other times

tightly held as the Colorado.

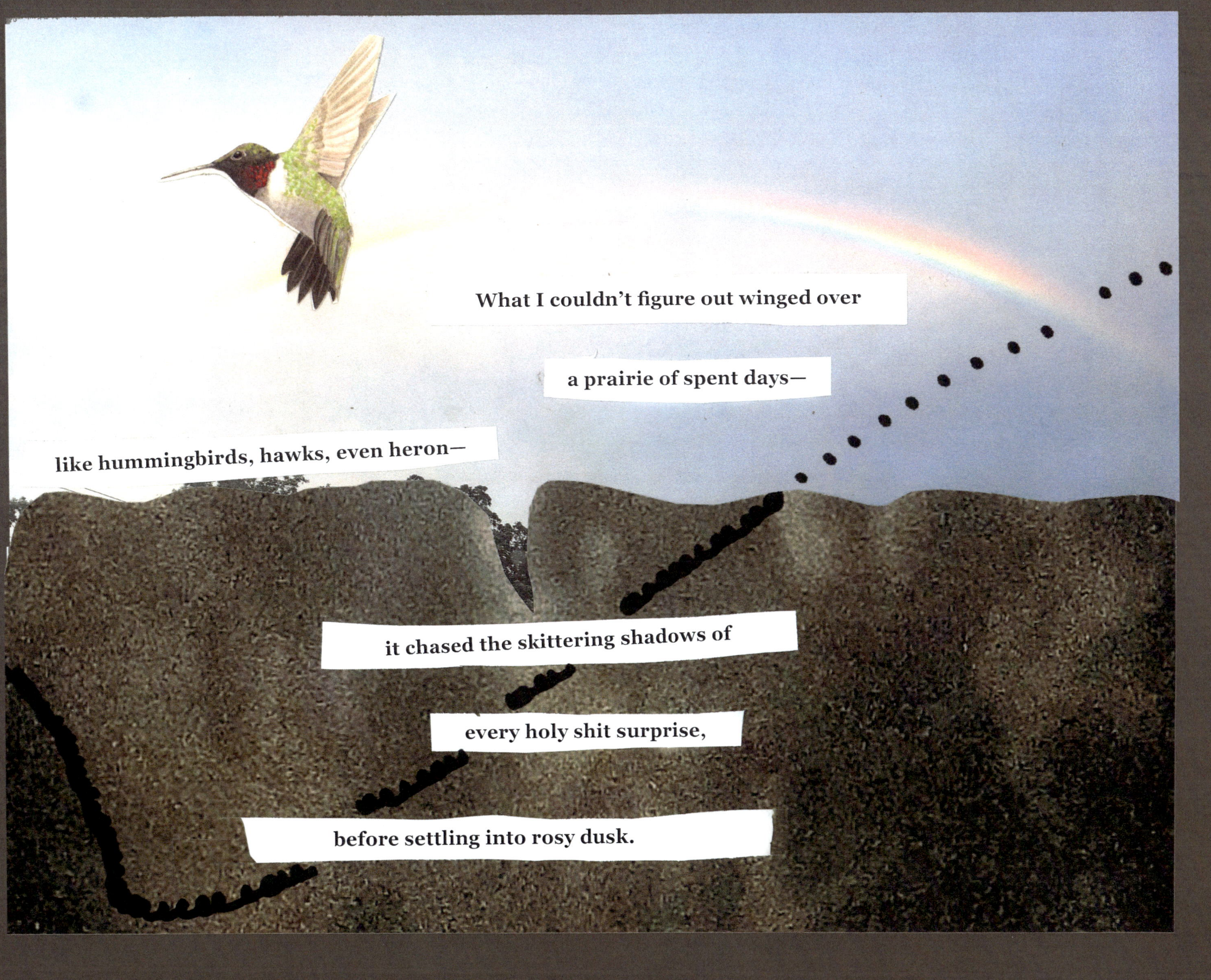
What I couldn't figure out winged over
a prairie of spent days—
like hummingbirds, hawks, even heron—
it chased the skittering shadows of
every holy shit surprise,
before settling into rosy dusk.

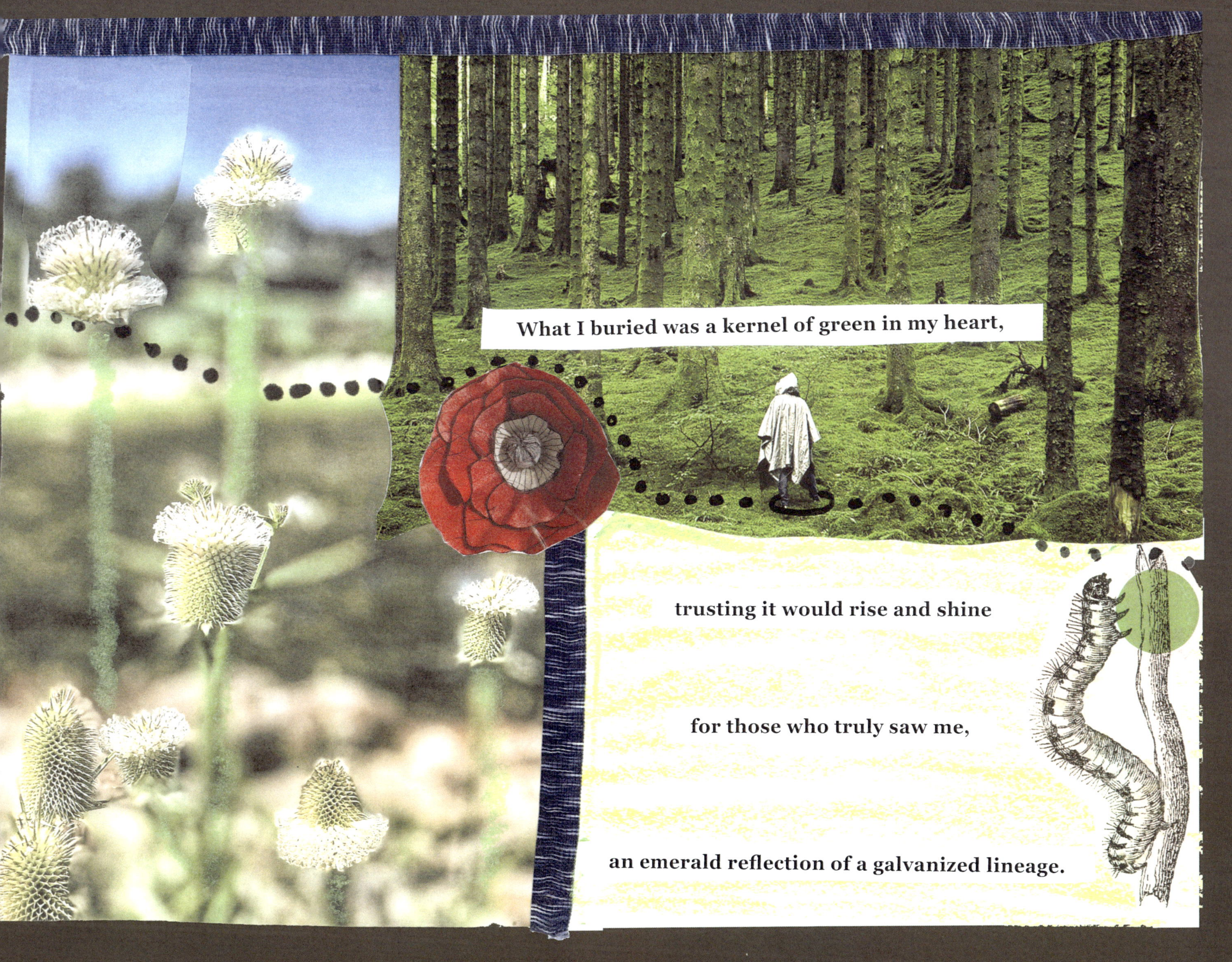
What I buried was a kernel of green in my heart,
trusting it would rise and shine
for those who truly saw me,
an emerald reflection of a galvanized lineage.

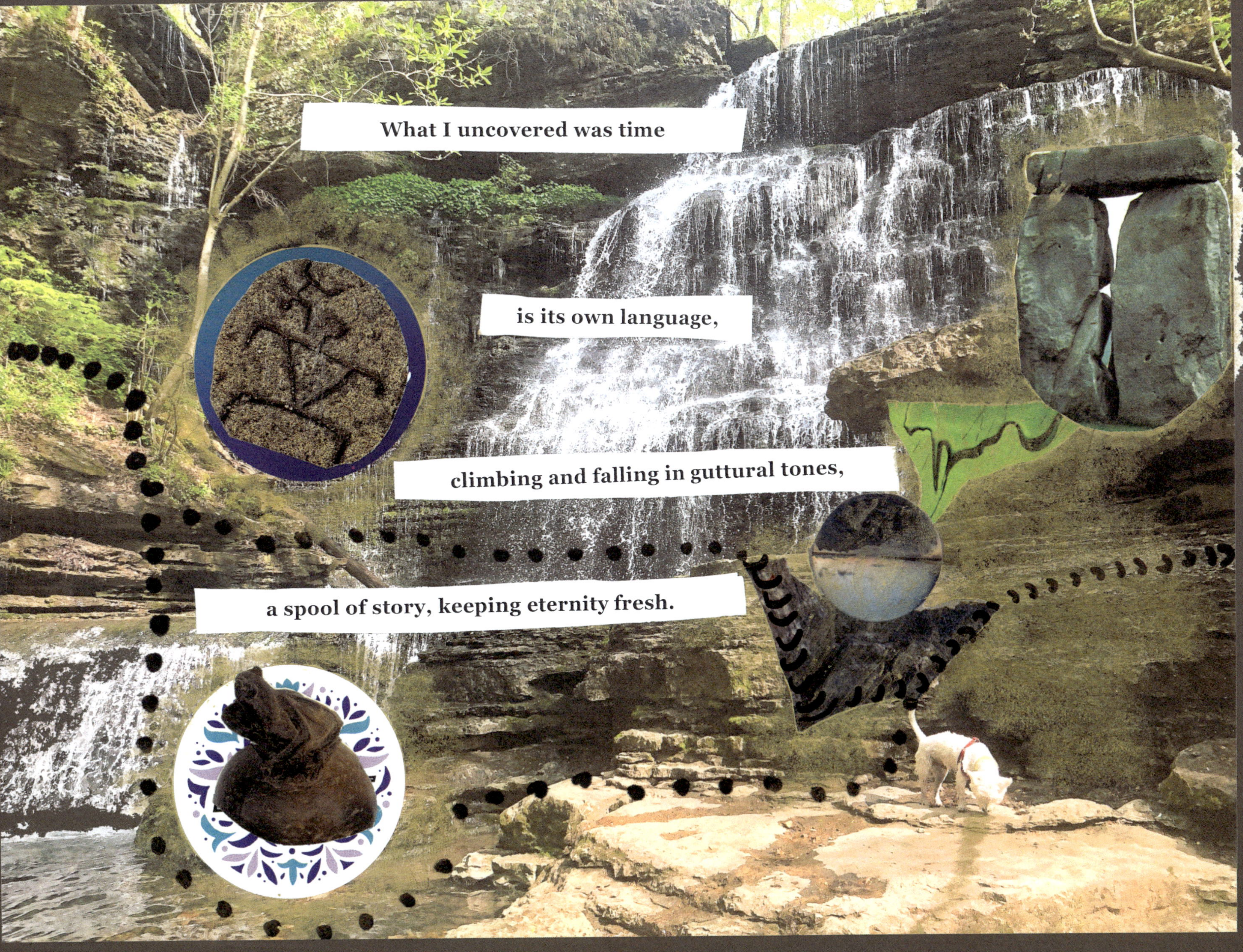
What I uncovered was time
is its own language,
climbing and falling in guttural tones,
a spool of story, keeping eternity fresh.

40

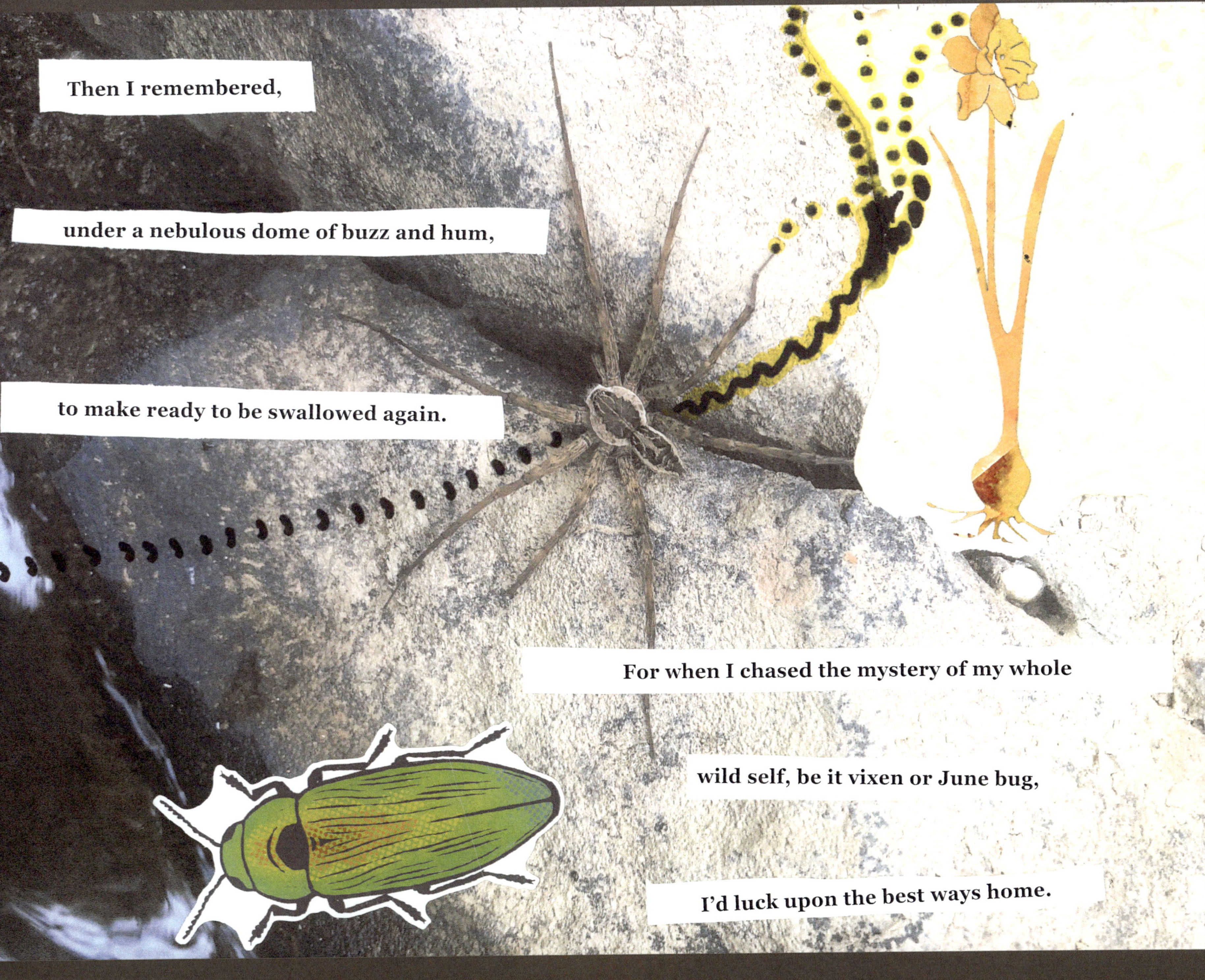
Then I remembered,
under a nebulous dome of buzz and hum,
to make ready to be swallowed again.
For when I chased the mystery of my whole
wild self, be it vixen or June bug,
I'd luck upon the best ways home.

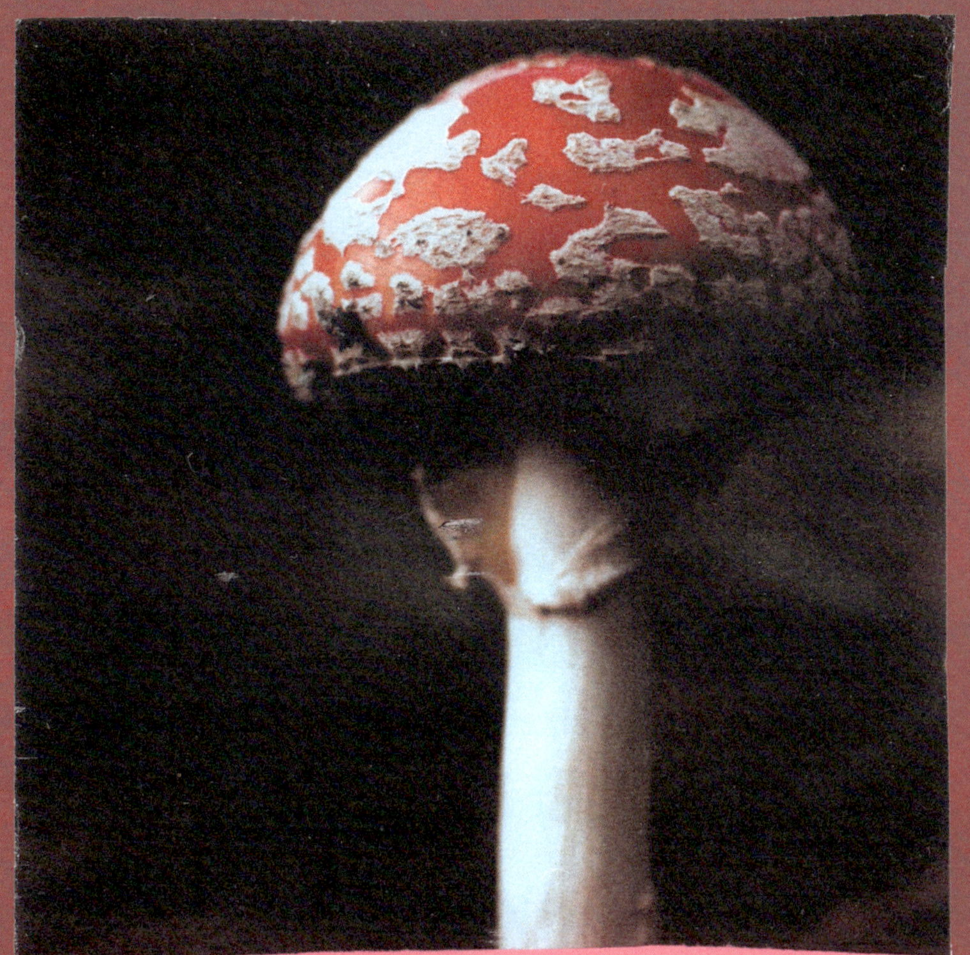

Composting Temples

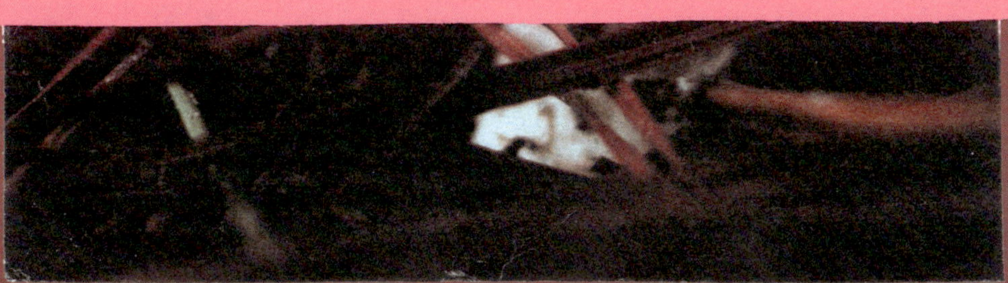

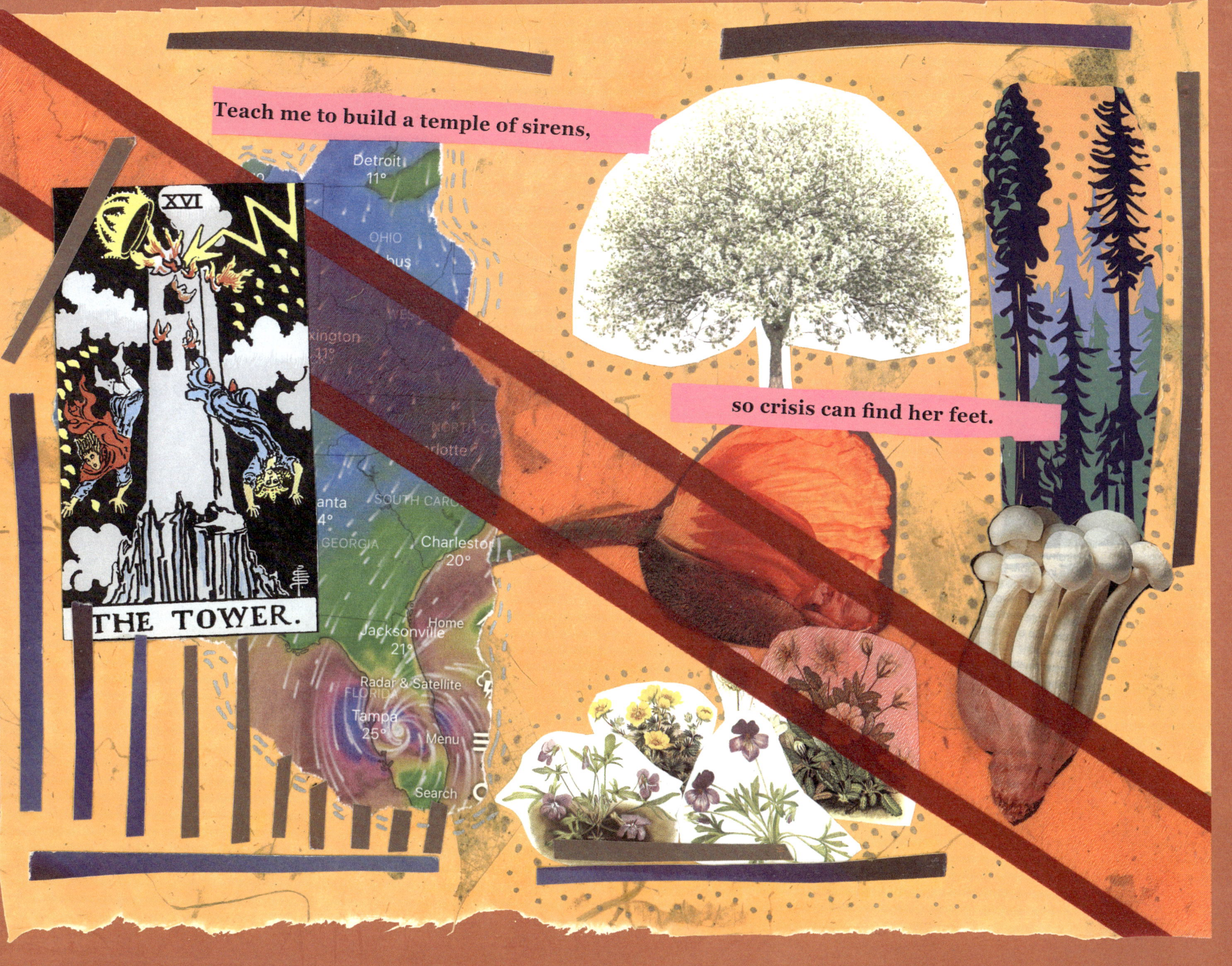
Teach me to build a temple of sirens,
so crisis can find her feet.
XVI
THE TOWER.
Detroit
11°
OHIO
GEORGIA
Charleston
20°
Home
Jacksonville
21°
Radar & Satellite
Tampa
25°
Menu
Search

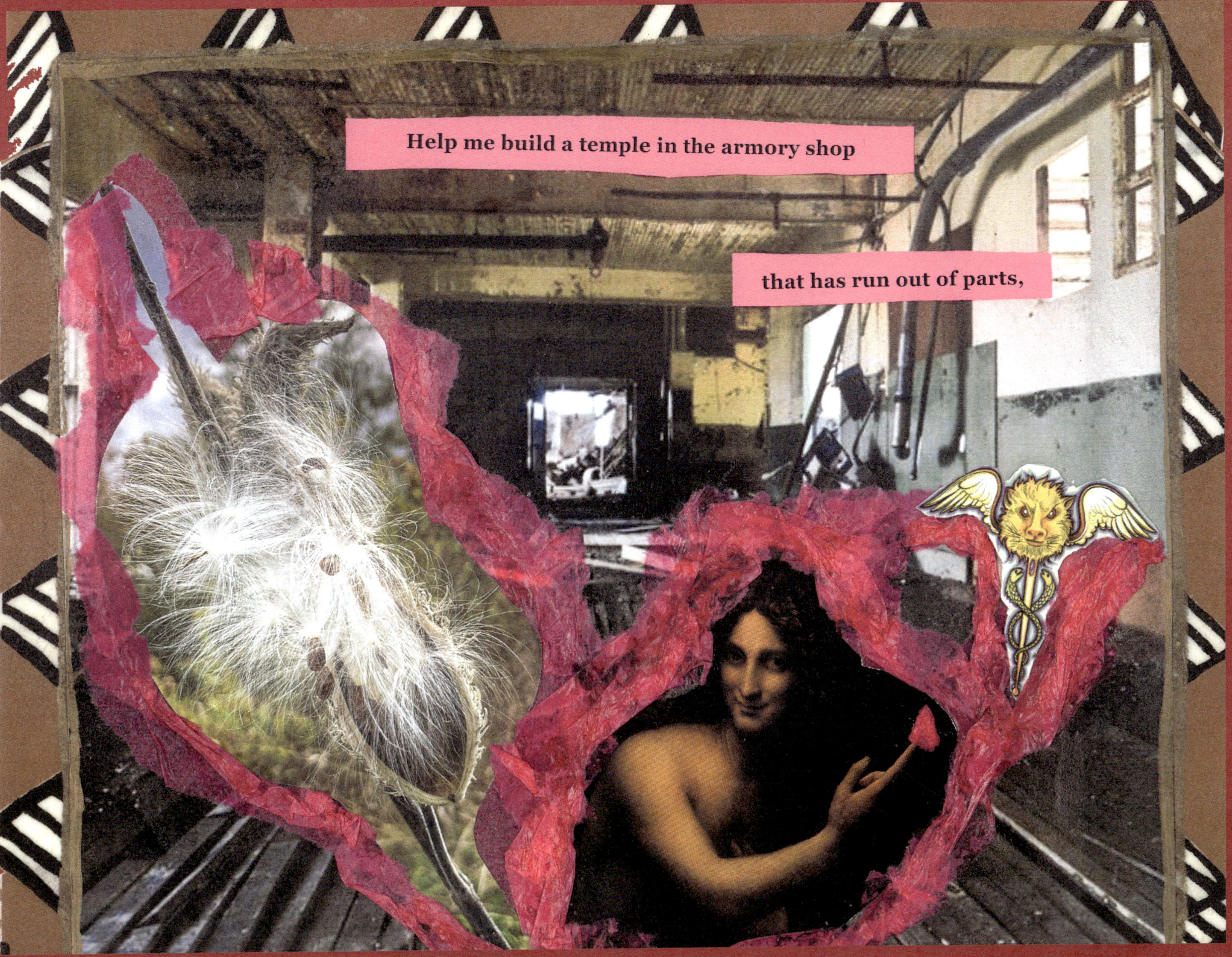
Help me build a temple in the armory shop
that has run out of parts,

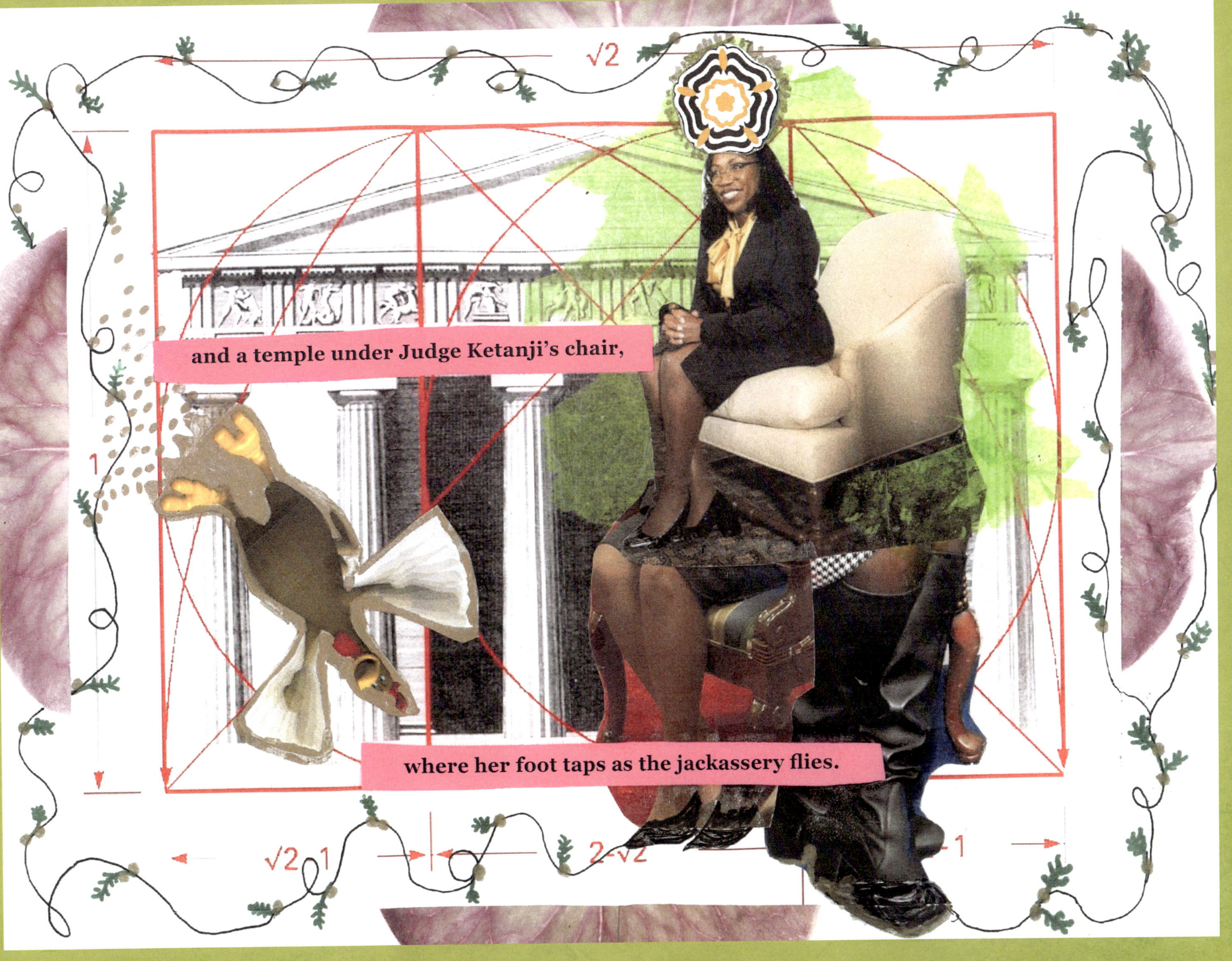
√2
and a temple under Judge Ketanji's chair,
1
1
where her foot taps as the jackassery flies.
√2
1
2-√2
1

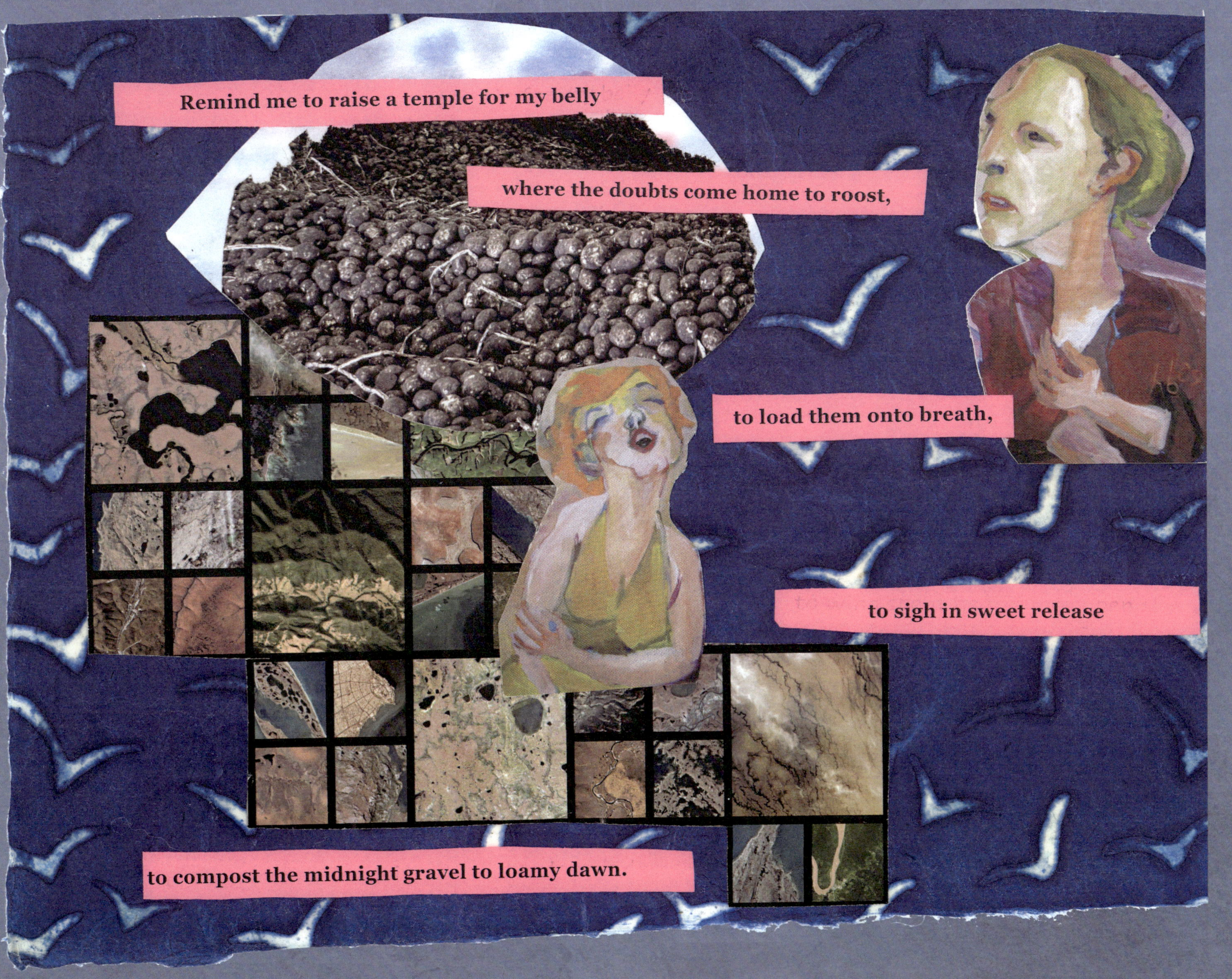
Remind me to raise a temple for my belly
where the doubts come home to roost,
to load them onto breath,
to sigh in sweet release
to compost the midnight gravel to loamy dawn.

52

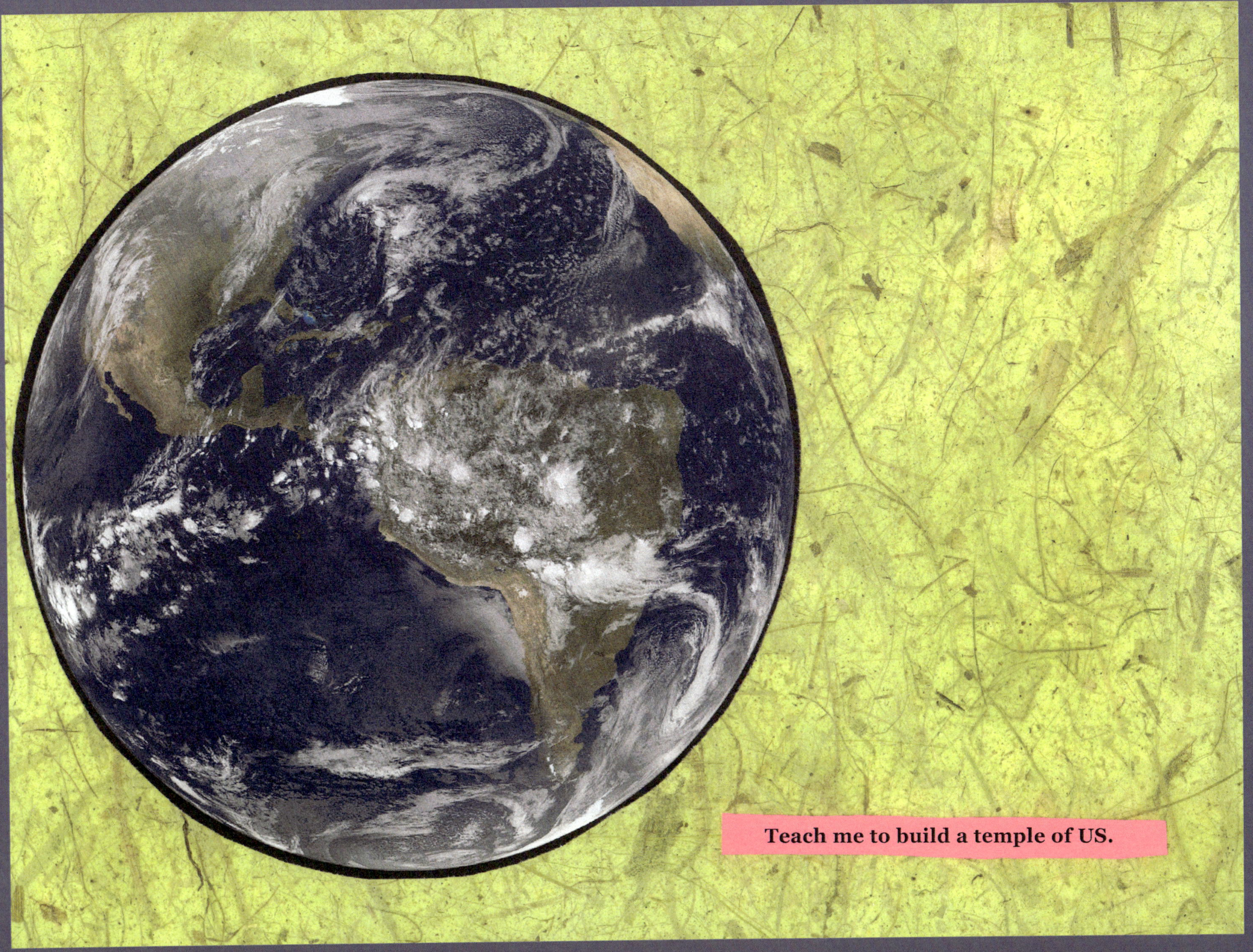
Teach me to build a temple of US.

Acknowledgments

Composting Temples is a project started in 2022 in the last months of my mother's life as I witnessed her crossing the hallowed ground between living and dying. I am very thankful to my siblings, Jill Crossley, Ellen, Laurie, and Rand Cimino, who shared the difficult and weighty obligation of saying goodbye to the one who birthed us. They helped me keep it together as we cared for her. And I hold huge gratitude for my mother, Althea Cimino, who celebrated with me the daily pages of this trilogy as I brought them to her bedside fresh from my worktable.

I commend my publishers at Wild Rising Press, Judyth Hill and Mary Meade, for their care and expertise in midwiving this book into the world with me.

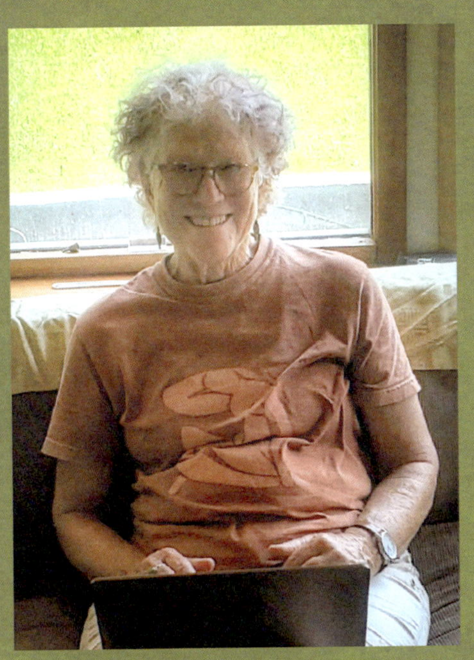

About the Author

RM mist is a queer hedge witch, artist, poet, and storyteller who resides among the Appalachian Mountains of North Carolina in the French Broad watershed with her soulmate and her Westie. She feeds her creative expression by exploring local ecologies, crafting, cooking, collaborating in human and natural communities, backcountry rambling, and writing.

She has published four chapbooks: Inviting Calamity, Ariadne's Passage, Hamsa Hamsa Hamsa, and The Transit of Venus (a collaborative ekphrastic volume of poems and paintings), as well as a recent poetry collection, When We Were Dragonflies.

Exquisite and perfectly befitting is the choice of Bodoni for the titles in *Composting Temples.* Named after its designer, Giambattista Bodoni (1740–1813), a leading Italian typographer known as the "King of Printers" for pushing the limits of printing technology. He pressed beauty into paper with hairline serifs and strokes so fine they seemed almost impossible. His groundbreaking typefaces, among the first true "modern serifs," displaced the softer "Old Face" and "Old Style" in use at the time. His influence on typography remained dominant until the end of the 19th century and inspires new creations to this day. Bodoni is famously said to embody the Enlightenment's embrace of rationality, reason, and innovation, challenging traditional authority, and ultimately, advocating for individual liberty and tolerance. Cool and elegant, with a subtext of innovation swept in on the fresh winds of science, Bodoni provides a marvelously apt introduction to the work in this poetry triptych's fusion of intellect and imagination. For the body text, the designer chose Georgia, Matthew Carter's generous, welcoming typeface. Where Bodoni is crystalline, Georgia is warm and supple, its curves offering quiet intimacy. Georgia beckons us closer, answering the crisp edge of Bodoni with its air of friendliness and ease —a voice leaning in to tell a secret, a sweet match to the poet's unique, playful, and evocative combination of text and image. The images in *Composting Temples* open lush and subliminal layers of meaning; tone and tenor twists and twirls as the words themselves shapeshift from verbal to visual and back, all the while the warmth of this font beckons us to enter and revel in the sassy wisdom of this poet's lyrical embrace of delicious mysteries.

www.ingramcontent.com/pod-product-compliance
Ingram Content Group UK Ltd.
Pitfield, Milton Keynes, MK11 3LW, UK
UKRC032326290726
14090UKWH00011B/497